D1549036

THE TEXAS NUTCRACKER

WRITTEN BY
JENNIFER COLEMAN

ILLUSTRATED BY
WADE DILLON

PELICAN PUBLISHING COMPANY

GRETNA 2018

The word "Pelican" and the depiction of a pelican are trademarks of Pelican Publishing Company, Inc., and are registered in the U.S. Patent and Trademark Office.

Library of Congress Cataloging-in-Publication Data

Names: Coleman, Jennifer, 1971- author. | Dillon, Wade, 1988- illustrator. |
  Hoffmann, E. T. A. (Ernst Theodor Amadeus), 1776-1822. Nussknacker und
Mauskönig.
Title: The Texas nutcracker / by Jennifer Coleman ; illustrated by Wade
  Dillon.
Description: Gretna : Pelican Publishing Company, 2018. | Summary: A version
  of the famous tale reset in Fort Davis, Texas, in 1883, in which young
  Centennia helps break the spell on her toy soldier nutcracker and watches
  it change into a handsome prince. Includes facts about Fort Davis.
Identifiers: LCCN 2018000561| ISBN 9781455623310 (alk. paper) | ISBN
  9781455623327 (ebook)
Subjects: | CYAC: Fairy tales. | Soldiers--Fiction. | Christmas--Fiction. |
  Fort Davis (Tex.)--Fiction. | Texas--History--1846-1950--Fiction.
Classification: LCC PZ8.C6827 Tex 2018 | DDC [E]--dc23 LC record available
at https://lccn.loc.gov/2018000561

Printed in Malaysia

Published by Pelican Publishing Company, Inc.
1000 Burmaster Street, Gretna, Louisiana 70053
www.pelicanpub.com

For Briana, Caroline, and Sam—JC
To the late Jeffery Dane, who loved music
and history—WD

"I can't wait for the party to start!" Centennia cried. It was the family's first Christmas at Fort Davis. Centennia and her brother Caleb strung ropes of cranberries to hang on their goose feather tree.

Fat snowflakes dusted the large cottonwood trees outside. *Brrrr,* the cold air swirled. Were snakes and coyotes napping in the mountains near her home at the fort?

Centennia twisted at a ring that her Papa had made for her himself. It fit her finger perfectly. Papa bent the nail of one of the shoes from a soldier's horse to make her ring. It felt fancy, like a fine jewel. At last the guests arrived! She turned her ring round and round her finger while Colonel Grierson carried in the presents. The children clapped their hands as he passed out shiny glass marbles.

Next, the Colonel bent down with a special gift. "This is for you, little Miss Centennia."
Centennia rocked a wooden nutcracker in her arms. It was the figure of a soldier with a snowy soft beard. What a fine officer! Centennia could not take her eyes off of him.

"Ugly old man!" Caleb called the nutcracker, "I bet he can't even crack a pecan!" Caleb grabbed a nearby nut and crammed it into the nutcracker's mouth. *Crack! Crack!* Two teeth fell out.

"Caleb! Stop! You're hurting him!"
Centennia snatched back her gift.
"You can have your broken
nutcracker. What good is a soldier
who can't do his job?" Caleb asked.

Centennia untied the sash on her hat and wrapped it around the soldier's jaw. "I'll protect you," she whispered.

Much later after all were in bed, Centennia creeped back into the parlor. She spied her nutcracker. Her chest hurt when she thought of Caleb's treatment of her present.

The mantel clock chimed. Centennia jumped at the sound!

The goose feather Christmas tree began growing bigger and bigger! The toys in the room grew along beside it. Now Centennia was no larger than the size of the nutcracker. What was happening?

Rattttttttle, Rattttttttttle.
The growing tree startled a den of slumbering rattlesnakes. An army of snakes came up through the floor cracks and slithered toward Centennia.

The biggest, a frightening Rattlesnake King, flicked his tongue. He beat his tail as he slid to the front of the heap.

Drums pounded. The other toys that had been around the tree in the room sprang into action. All at once, the nutcracker leaped forward, wielding his sword.

Centennia froze in shock—her beloved nutcracker and his small toy army drove back the pack of rattlesnakes.

Rattttttttle, Rattttttttttle.
A snake struck out and stripped the nutcracker solider of his sword. "Why have you disturbed our sssssleeep?" hissed the Rattlesnake King. The snake coiled to strike.

"No! Stop!" Centennia yanked off her ring, throwing it with all her might. The hard ring hit the snake between the eyes. In a flash, the mass of snakes disappeared as if by magic.

Just then the nutcracker changed into a handsome cavalry soldier. "Oh," he said taking a knee, "you have saved me! With my thanks, be my guest at my true home—The Land of the Wildflowers."

Leading her by the hand, he guided
Centennia to a chuck wagon outside.
The crisp night air felt electric.

After a short star and moonlit journey, a stunning lady in blue greeted Centennia and the soldier.

"May I introduce the Bluebonnet Fairy," the soldier said. He told the Bluebonnet Fairy of his battle with the Rattlesnake King, and how Centennia saved his life.

The Bluebonnet Fairy kissed Centennia's cheek. She waved her hands and a flock of Monarch butterflies fluttered in a homecoming dance to honor the soldier's return. "Now, let us feast in celebration!"

The soldier led Centennia through a bluebonnet maze into a grand, white pueblo.

As they feasted on chili con carne, Centennia and the prince were treated to one lively dance after another.

A flurry of horned lizards jumped, darted, and bowed.

The Dance of the Mockingbirds was so fast; Centennia didn't know where to look!

Next a band of funny armadillos performed a square dance called "Cotton Eyed Joe."

Then all of the flowers of the meadows gathered for the Waltz of the Wildflowers. The Bluebonnet Fairy led it herself. Centennia marveled at the colorful dances though it was soon time to go.

Centennia and her nutcracker prince stepped back into the wagon. Everyone waved goodbye.

Before she knew it, Centennia was tucked in her own quilt-covered bed. She did not mention to anyone her journey to the Land of the Wildflowers, not even to Caleb.

Centennia knew in her heart that one day she would return back to the magical place with the nutcracker she loved. Extraordinary things awaited those with eyes as wide as the Texas skies.

Author's Note

Fort Davis Facts

From 1854 to 1891 (except during the time of the Civil War), men of the United States Army built and maintained Fort Davis near the Davis Mountains in West Texas. Soldiers at the Fort helped to build a new and shorter road between San Antonio and Fort Davis. The fort was also a help to those building railroads across the country. Today the remains of Fort Davis honor an important chapter in the making of the American frontier.

Words to Know

Centennia—A female name popular in this time, probably chosen to honor The United States of America's 100th birthday, or the centennial, 1876.

Colonel Benjamin Grierson—A gifted musician who became an important army officer during the time of the Civil War. During the 1880s, Grierson commanded the Departments of Texas, New Mexico, and Arizona. Fort Davis was one of his many commands. He was also a part of the Buffalo soldiers, which was part of the U.S. Army from 1867 to 1896.

Goose feather tree—Goose feathers were plentiful and easily made into Christmas trees. Feathers were dyed green and wired to wooden sticks that were made into the shape of a tree. Red berries were usually placed onto the ends of branches. Real candles were used to light the tree!